better together*

* This book is best read together, grownup and kid.

a
kids
book
about

a kids book about PETS & LOVE

by Taylor Hill

A Kids Book About
Editor Emma Wolf
Head of Design Rick DeLucco
Publisher Jelani Memory

DK
Senior Production Editor Jennifer Murray
Senior Production Controller Louise Minihane
Managing Editor Hazel Eriksson
Publishing Director Mark Searle

This American Edition, 2025
Published in the United States by DK Publishing,
a Division of Penguin Random House LLC
1745 Broadway, 20th Floor, New York, NY 10019

Text and design copyright © 2025 by A Kids Book About, Inc.
'A Kids Book About' is a trademark of Dorling Kindersley Ltd.
'Kids Are Ready' and the colophon 'a' are trademarks of A Kids Co.
25 26 27 28 29 10 9 8 7 6 5 4 3 2 1
001—356755—Nov/2025

All rights reserved. Without limiting the rights under the copyright reserved above, no part of this publication may be reproduced, stored in or introduced into a retrieval system, or transmitted, in any form, or by any means (electronic, mechanical, photocopying, recording, or otherwise), without the prior written permission of the copyright owner.

No part of this publication may be used or reproduced in any manner for the purpose of training artificial intelligence technologies or systems. In accordance with Article 4(3) of the DSM Directive 2019/790, DK expressly reserves this work from the text and data mining exception.

Published in Great Britain by Dorling Kindersley Limited.

ISBN 979-8-2171-3777-0

DK books are available at special discounts when purchased in bulk for sales promotions, premiums, fund-raising, or educational use. For details, contact: DK Publishing Special Markets, 1745 Broadway, 20th Floor, New York, NY 10019, or SpecialSales@dk.com

Printed and bound in China

Illustrations by Della Hu www.dellahu.cargo.site

www.dk.com

akidsco.com

This book was made with Forest Stewardship Council™ certified paper – one small step in DK's commitment to a sustainable future.
Learn more at www.dk.com/uk/information/sustainability

In memory of my sweet angel, Tate.

I carry you with me always.

Intro
for grownups

My dog Tate was a miniature labradoodle who was my most special companion. I got him when I was only 18 years old, and he was by my side for some of the most pivotal years of my life. It is only now that I truly appreciate how much I learned from him, and how valuable those lessons were.

I was not prepared for the grief I would feel when he died. I hope this book helps kids appreciate how special our relationships with pets can be, how much we can learn from them, and how to cope with the loss we feel when they inevitably leave us.

MY LOVE STARTED WHEN

FOR ANIMALS*.
I WAS A CHILD.

When I was 5,
we got our first family dog.

MAGGIE—we were so obsessed with her, and she wanted nothing to do with us!

My siblings and I were just 4 small kids, completely bombarding this little dog with affection.

Having a dog at a young age taught me how to

I can't remember who I was friends with when I was little, but I remember Maggie.

She helped me

LEARN CHORES,

RESPONSIBILITY,

AND WHY IT'S IMPORTANT TO TAKE CARE OF THINGS OTHER THAN OURSELVES.

When Maggie was 5,
she had a stroke.

My mom did a great job
of explaining what happened
to Maggie and what she
needed to heal.

Watching Maggie overcome
something so scary and seeing
her resilience was amazing.

As a teenager, my life was pretty different from other kids my age.

I was a model, travelling all over the world, which was really cool!

But I didn't get to spend a lot of time with friends, doing what other high schoolers do.

By the age of 18, I was living on my own in New York and I was lonely.

I FELT DISCONNECTED,

like something was
missing from my life.

So what did I do?

I got a dog,
I named him **TATE**
(after my grandpa).

AND HE CHANGED

MY LIFE FOREVER.

From the moment I met this miniature labradoodle, with the softest curls and sweetest eyes,

I KNEW HE WAS

MEANT FOR ME.

I was a young adult,
learning what it meant to
transition out of being a kid.

And Tate taught me...

PATIENCE,

KINDNESS,

EMOTIONAL SUPPORT,

AND THE KIND OF LOVE I DESERVE.

HE LOVED ME FOR ME.

Pets don't care about what your job is, how much money you make, or how popular you are.

THEY JUST LOVE YOU FOR THE REL

ATIONSHIP YOU HAVE WITH THEM.

I BELONGED TO TATE, AND HE BELONGED TO ME.

He came with me everywhere I went, and he made me feel safe when I was working with new people.

Tate was with me through some
of the toughest times of my life.

And he would look at me,
and I just knew **HE** knew I was
hurting and I needed him.

OUR PETS ARE SO SPECIAL.

They spend their whole lives loving us and growing with us...

BUT THEY AREN'T

HERE FOREVER.

Knowing that a day will come where you have to say goodbye is hard.

That day came sooner for me than I could have imagined.

IT WAS THE WEEK I WAS GETTING MARRIED, TATE WAS 9 YEARS OLD AND HE WASN'T DOING WELL.

We took him to the hospital
and he was diagnosed with
T-cell lymphoma—a really
aggressive kind of cancer.

I sat with him days before
I was supposed to travel for my
wedding and said to him,

"IF YOU NEED TO GO, YOU CAN.

JUST LET ME KNOW WHAT YOU NEED."

When it comes to our pets,
we can be selfish sometimes.

WE WANT THEM TO BE WITH US FOREVER! WE NEVER WANT THEM TO LEAVE.

But I needed Tate to know that I wanted what he needed, even if that meant letting him go.

However...the doctors gave him some medicine and within hours, he was a totally different dog!

He was awake, walking around, wagging his little tail.

I couldn't believe it,
and I was **SO** grateful.

WE HAD A BEAUTIFUL WEDDING WEEKEND, FULL OF LOVE, AND TATE WAS PART OF ALL OF IT.

WHEN WE GOT HOME, TATE CONTINUED WITH HIS CANCER TREATMENT, BUT IT WOULDN'T WORK FOREVER.

In fact, it only worked
for a few more weeks.

His cancer was back, more
aggressive than ever, and it was
attacking other parts of his body.

I truly believe he gave his all to be with me through one of the most special moments of my life, but now...

HE WAS READY TO GO. AND I HAD TO HONOR THAT.

My husband and I were able to do humane euthanasia* at our home.

Euthanasia is the painless killing of an animal who is suffering from an incurable disease or condition.

I could be with Tate through it all, and he didn't have to feel afraid of going back to the hospital.

I HELD HIM IN MY ARMS, TOLD HIM HOW MUCH I LOVED HIM, AND GOT TO SAY GOODBYE.

When he died, it felt really

And once he died, I experienced something massive called grief.

GRIEF IS WHEN YOU REALLY MISS SOMEONE WHO HAS DIED.

Every day, I was reminded
that he was gone.

I missed coming through
the front door and seeing
him run toward me.

The time I had with Tate
is something I'll cherish
for the rest of my life.

HE'S IMPACTED MY LIFE IN SO MANY WAYS.

As I'm writing this,
I lost Tate 2 years ago,
and I still think of
him every day.

I THINK OF GRIEF LIKE AN OCEAN.

Sometimes, it's calm and peaceful, and you can just float along with it.

But other times, the waves are crashing, and it feels almost impossible to stay above water.

BE PATIENT WITH YOUR GRIEF.

It’ll come and go, and it’s
best to just let it exist.

Death is scary, tragic, and sad.

BUT WITH TIME, BEAUTIFUL

THINGS CAN COME FROM PAIN.

While Tate might physically be gone, I see him in my life all the time.

I CARRY HIS MEMORY, HIS LOVE, AND HIS JOY

with me wherever I go.

Outro
for grownups

If you've ever loved a pet—or had to say goodbye to one—this book is for you. Pets are some of our greatest teachers. They show us how to love fully, be present, and care for someone other than ourselves. And when they leave us, they remind us just how deep love can go.

Losing a pet is one of the hardest things we can go through, no matter how old we are. It's OK to feel sad. It's OK to cry. And it's OK to miss them for a long, long time.

This story is about my dog Tate and all the love he gave me, and it's also about grief, healing, and holding on to memories that never fade.

I hope it helps you feel less alone.
I hope it helps you celebrate your pet.
And I hope it reminds you that love, even after loss, never really goes away.

About The Author

Taylor Hill (she/her) is an internationally renowned supermodel, actress, and entrepreneur. She began her career at the age of 14 and rose to global fame as a Victoria's Secret Angel. She has appeared on countless editorial covers for publications including *Vogue*, *Elle*, and *Harper's Bazaar*, and has worked with some of the most recognizable global brands, including Chanel, David Yurman, and Ralph Lauren.

Taylor is a passionate advocate for the human-animal bond. She is the founder and CEO of Tate & Taylor, a media and retail platform celebrating life with pets, and proudly serves as Honorary Chair of Young Friends at the Schwarzman Animal Medical Center.

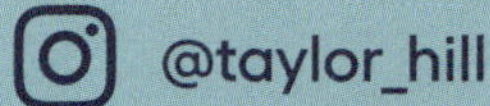

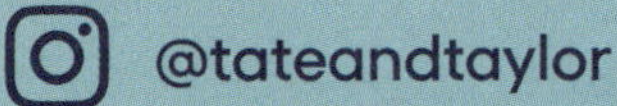

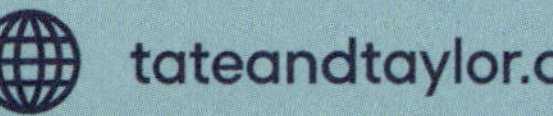

Made to empower.

Discover more at akidsco.com